The Mammoth Book of

THE FUNNIEST CARTOONS OF ALL TIME

Also available

The Mammoth Book of

THE FUNNIEST CARTOONS
OF ALL TIME

Edited by Geoff Tibballs

CARROLL & GRAF PUBLISHERS
New York

Carroll & Graf Publishers
An imprint of Avalon Publishing Group, Inc.
245 W. 17th Street
11th Floor
New York, NY 10011-5300
www.carrollandgraf.com

AVALON
publishing group incorporated

First Carroll & Graf edition 2006

First published in the UK by Robinson,
an imprint of Constable & Robinson Ltd 2006

ISBN-13: 978-0-78671-831-3
ISBN-10: 0-7867-1831-5

Printed and bound in the EU

CONTENTS

INTRODUCTION

Some people howl with laughter at the sight of slapstick comedy. Others prefer deadpan delivery. I've always had a weakness for talking dogs.

Animals with human characteristics have long been a favourite with cartoonists. The concept underlines the power of the cartoonist's pen – an ability to break all the rules and create a surreal world. For centuries the cartoon has been an essential art form, part of the very fabric of society. At one end of the spectrum it can be bitingly satirical, lampooning eminent figures and causing welcome embarrassment to statesmen, politicians and their fellow wastrels; at the other it provides a humorous reflection on the absurdities of everyday life, sometimes straying into that strange world where animals read newspapers and complain about the price of dog food in the supermarket.

This collection of over 400 of the world's funniest cartoons from the last seventy years or so offers a running commentary on our ever-changing society. All the usual suspects are here: the malevolent dentist, the pompous boss, the frustrated housewife, the lazy husband and the nosey neighbour. It is interesting to note how the depictions of these stereotypes have altered down the decades. Today the dentist is more likely to be concerned with profit margins than inflicting pain, the old-style boss has been laid off and replaced by a young thrusting type with a GCSE in Business Management, the housewife runs a multinational company, the lazy husband has made chief constable while the nosey neighbour is probably into dogging.

Most of the leading cartoonists are featured in this book, names like Mac, Larry, Matt, ffolkes, Charles Barsotti, Gerard Hoffnung, Bill Tidy and William Haefeli each putting a highly individual slant on everything from Death to DIY, Art to Aliens and Science to Sport. Generally speaking, anything too topical has been excluded in favour of timeless classics.

As I hope is apparent from this selection, a good cartoon is more than just an illustrated joke. Study the contrasting styles and look out for such ingredients as facial expressions and background detail. For a finely crafted cartoon can be as intricate as a Constable or a Lowry – and usually with a better punchline. I only wish I could think of one to end this introduction.

Geoff Tibballs, February 2006

ANIMALS AND PETS

SCHWADRON

"You see? He's a different dog when he smiles."

John Donegan

"Lot 64. What am I bid?"

Norman Thelwell

"Nothing personal, Pooh, but we figured you'd fetch a
fortune on the open market."

Alan de la Nougerede

"You've overdone the aftershave again."

Michael Heath

"I must say, Mr Baskerville, we had expected
something larger."

Michael ffolkes (Brian Davis)

"What he lacks in conversation, he makes up for in storage space."

David Haldane

"Boy! What a party!"

William Hewison

"Sorry about that – he's allergic to cats."

Holte (Trevor Holder)

"We've decided against divorce. Neither of us wants
custody of the dog."

Michael ffolkes (Brian Davis)

"Strange, you don't usually see seagulls this far inland."

Martin Honeysett

"Look what the cat's dragged in!"

Les Barton

"The only thing 'wrong' about Tarquin, Mrs Millhouse, is that he isn't an Old English Sheep-dog. He's an Old English ant-eater."

John Donegan

"My God! Gramophone-sniffing!"

Ed McLachlan

"Your wife wants to know if you'll agree to have him put down."

David Myers

"Here's my card. It has an area that you can scratch and sniff."

Harley Schwadron

"That was funny when he said he'd get his big brother."

Tony Husband

"…upper right seven buccal filling…upper right six mesial filling
with palatal extension…"

Mike Williams

"Oh, hell! Are you sure? I was hoping we were Lust."

Bud Handelsman

"Is it spring already?"

Ed McLachlan

"Let's up that thermostat a notch or two, buddy boy.
Remember, Polly is a tropical bird."

Henry Martin

"What are you wagging your tail at, you cheerful bastard?"

Tony Husband

"It's spring all right – the tortoise is awake!"

Holte (Trevor Holder)

"Why wait till Father's Day? Give it to him now."

John Donegan

"And to my faithful and devoted pets I leave the residue of…"

Anton (Beryl Antonia Yeoman)

"As far as I'm concerned he could stay out all night."

Martin Honeysett

"It's at about seventy I get this funny knocking noise."

Mike Williams

"Please...I don't want to hear any more about your rotten childhood."

Tom Cheney

"I must say the sloths are taking it extremely well."

Banx (Jeremy Banks)

"You're noisy for a cat."

Frank Cotham

ART

"Your perspective's a bit out."

Vernon Kirby

"Bloody hell, Mavis! The bus leaves in ten minutes."

Bud Grace

"Are you any good at untying knots?"

Michael ffolkes (Brian Davis)

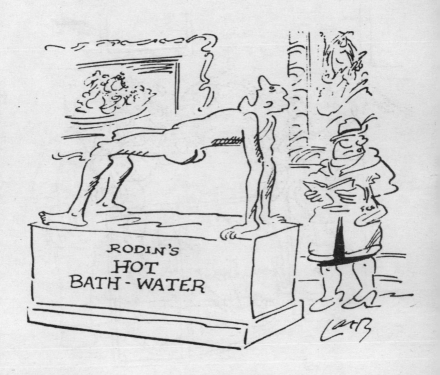

RODIN'S
HOT
BATH-WATER

Larry (Terry Parkes)

"I'm afraid it's a fake"

Joel Mishon

"He really captured her in this one."

Mike Baldwin

Larry (Terry Parkes)

Stan Eales

BUSINESS AND WORK

"It's several weeks too early – I hadn't finished complaining about the drought."

Sally Artz

Frank Cotham

"Oh, come in and give me your 'I-don't-resent-you-for-being-a-woman' look, will you, Mr Saunders?"

Nick Baker

"Do you think the directors ever pretend to be us?"

Hector Breeze

"Terrible! You always think somehow that it can
never happen to you."

Frank Cotham

"Don't be daft. It's the only place in the building
where he can have a smoke."

Riana Duncan

Hector Breeze

"Lip service, please."

John Donegan

"Whatever it turns out to be, rush it to production."

Charles Barsotti

"My family? Hell no, those are my clients."

Stan Eales

"The fact is, Mr Wetherby, we're looking for someone who can take it. We're already well supplied with those who can dish it out."

Riana Duncan

"Let's put it this way, Mr Greame: every man's conscience has its over-ride button."

Ed Fisher

"That's my advice as your accountant.
Speaking as your friend, I'd have to say it was pretty
lousy advice."

Bud Handelsman

"Tell me, Smithers, if all the world's a stage, how come all the clowns are employed in this office?"

Riana Duncan

"Good morning, sir! I represent Rupert Murdoch. We bought a
controlling interest in you as you slept."

Bud Handelsman

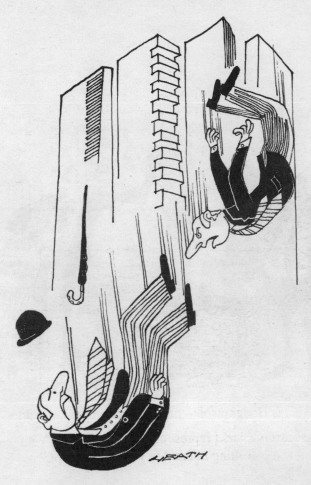

"Thanks for the advice."

Michael Heath

"This is Hodgkinson – he's in charge of the shredder"

Holte (Trevor Holder)

"It was 1961. Boom times, stability, easy credit…and, of course, none of the other entering classmen at law school thought of specializing in insolvency cases."

Ed Fisher

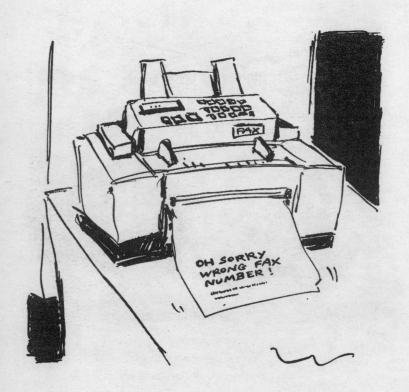

Steve Way

"Good grief! This balance-sheet won't do – why damn it,
a child could understand it."

William Scully

"It's the boss's idea – Benton's the best worker in the office."

David Myers

"I just want to say that this is the best Board of Directors I've ever been on, and I hope we can all stay friends for ever and ever."

Sidney Harris

Ed McLachlan

"Mr Jalton, I think we're about to be wooed by Apex Ltd."

Henry Martin

"Behind the plotting and scheming in every office, there is someone doing the actual work and that someone, Rogers, better be you."

Henry Martin

"Six thousand a year may not sound much,
but look at it this way."

John Donegan

"I see it as a golden opportunity for you to tighten your stranglehold on me."

John Donegan

"I want you to go to the Personnel Director and bite him,
then go to Sales and bite Hempstead and Beasly,
then trot on down to Bookkeeping…"

Frank Cotham

"Look at it this way, Mr Helfrick – the sun is shining, the birds are singing, the bees are humming, inflation is spiralling and the flowers are bloomimg. Four out of five isn't bad."

Henry Martin

"I love the absolute power that goes with my job.
It allows me to be myself."

Frank Cotham

"J.B. has just had this marvellous brainwave –
we'll use your idea!"

Albert (Albert Rusling)

"I can't decide what to wear for the office party."

Riana Duncan

"I want you to know, Nettleson, how much I appreciate your sticking by me now that things have got tough."

Frank Cotham

"I often think how nice it would be to have enough imagination to live in a dream world."

Ken Pyne

"There are, however, some disadvantages to being self-employed."

Martin Honeysett

Tony Husband

"First, I'd like to propose that we move a vote of thanks that the whole of the committee escaped the shipwreck."

Ray Lowry

"Ed, next year when I reach retirement – please! No fanfare. No banquet. No speeches. No silver tray. I just want to slip out quietly with my old attaché case full of big ones."

Henry Martin

"First off, forget I'm a woman."

Rip Matteson

"They're on to us!"

Frank Cotham

"He's a glutton for work – that's as close as he ever gets to a holiday."

David Myers

"And Clive will always be remembered as the most hard-working member of the sales team."

David Haldane

"Scope for advancement? I'll say. Take me, for instance.
I first came to this store as a shoplifter."

Sam Smith

"Apart from bossy, what other qualifications have you?"

William Scully

"Sorry to be the bearer of bad tidings, Thigben, but your retirement was a computer error."

Harley Schwadron

"Is there some way you could help me, but make
it look like I did it all myself?"

Frank Cotham

"See here, Potter, why can't you grovel for a raise
like everyone else?"

Harley Schwadron

"As soon as my nail varnish is dry I'm going to claw
my way to the top."

Merrily Harpur

"Let me just make one thing clear, Henderson –
if I needed your opinion, I'd fire you."

Ken Pyne

CHILDREN

"One by one, they all grew up…left
home…married…divorced…came drifting back…"

Sally Artz

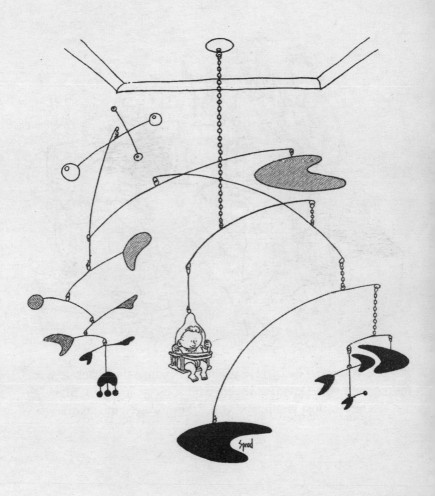

George Sprod

"Since you ask, I had you, Samantha, because the birthrate was falling; and you, David, as revenge on society; and you, Mark, as a bid for lost youth; and you, Jason, were a mistake."

Merrily Harpur

"Oi! Can't you read?"

Tony Husband

"The children just don't seem to confide in us any more."

Anton (Beryl Antonia Yeoman)

"Yes, Darling! Mummy has to keep her hands lovely in case she ever wants to go back to brain surgery."

Merrily Harpur

"Oh, by the way…according to my teacher I'm suffering from a lack of discipline in the home. See to it, will you…?"

Clive Collins

"…And to my children I leave the name of their real father!"

Pete Dredge

"I hope the children aren't bothering you."

Martin Honeysett

"That reminds me – the strap broke on ours.
I must get it repaired."

Tony Husband

"I don't think it's to do with your begetting an infant prodigy, dad, so much as it's to do with your being stupid."

Vernon Kirby

J.W. Taylor

Steve Way

CHRISTMAS

"Oh really? I was thinking of calling mine Santa Claus."

Stan McMurtry

"It's only my father, he'll be gone in a minute."

Michael Heath

"You don't mind, do you, Vicar? It's the only place where you can escape from Christmas for a few minutes."

Tony Holland

Roy Davis

"Why can't we have what we had last year – leg?"

Stan McMurtry

"Mummy! Mummy! Daddy's batteries have run out!"

Michael Heath

"You'll never regret this – he was a pretty dumb parrot."

Stan McMurtry

"It's the Easter Bunny. Do we want to discuss
the possibility of a merger?"

Harley Schwadron

"We can't, it would spoil our working relationship."

Robert Thompson

"Miss Gardner, tell the staff they can come in quietly, one at a time, and have a look at my Christmas tree."

Colin Whittock

"Ah Christmas, the unmistakable aroma of pine-needles, infused with the myriad piquant fragrances of seasonal comfort and joy."

Holte (Trevor Holder)

"Stop moaning – we were at your parents' last year!"

Stan McMurtry

COMPUTERS

"Hello, tech support? I can't seem to remove the icons from my desktop."

Thomas Bros.

COMPUTERS

"I shall now hand over to our guest speaker, management unit XT-56."

Naf (Andy McKay)

COMPUTERS

"Know what I really miss? Office rumours."

Nick (Nick Hobart)

"Ms Johnson, would you mind ordering me another computer? And you can cancel that call to tech-support."

Jerry King

"I love the fact that you're a computer genius, Erwin. I just don't like the fact that you look like one."

Jerry King

"Here's your problem – the batteries are in upside down."

Harley Schwadron

"Know what really chokes me? That £50,000
computer I stole now sells for £69.95."

Nick (Nick Hobart)

"Now I don't feel so guilty about drinking to forget. I stored everything I know on the computer."

Harley Schwadron

"I just wanted to thank you for grounding me to my room for the weekend. I took the time to start a computer programming company, which earned me $13 million."

Jerry King

COMPUTERS

Mike Baldwin

"Just show me the mouse."

Harley Schwadron

"When you say you have a terminal malfunction, Jackson,
I trust you are speaking of yourself and not that five thousand
pounds' worth of new hardware in your office."

J.W. Taylor

"Mark my word Walters, this is no ordinary virus."

Ralph Hagen

Computer dating.

Gilligan

"Behold – an efficient information retrieval system,
with on-line access to stored detail…"

Alan de la Nougerede

DEATH AND FUNERALS

"Looks like he died of natural causes."

Mike Baldwin

"Bloody salesmen always give us trouble."

Nick Newman

"Are you sure this is what he meant by a quiet funeral?"

Fran Orford

"I haven't felt this important in years!"

Ken Pyne

"You know the rules, Mr Dotterill – you're
only allowed one visitor at a time."

Ed McLachlan

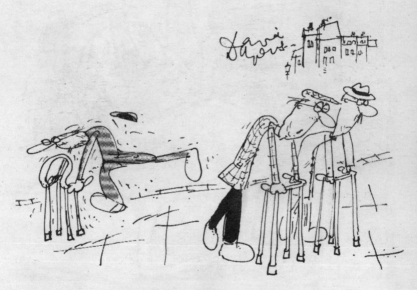

"It's the drop-handlebar sports model."

David Myers

"He won the right to die without dignity."

Mike Baldwin

"Well, I say one club's length from the ball
with a one stroke penalty."

Stan McMurtry

The eulogy was beautiful, although the question-answer period was rather odd.

Mike Baldwin

"He didn't want anything elaborate."

Martin Honeysett

DIY

"It's always the same, you get your first coat on,
and then loads of insects get bloody stuck to it."

Martin Ross

A botched home improvement job.

David Brown

"So that's where the spanner went."

Joseph Mirachi

"I'm going to put some shelves up. Certain scenes
may contain adult language."

Knife (Duncan McCoshan)

"He'll be here in a minute – he's just putting
up some shelves in the kitchen."

Holte (Trevor Holder)

Grizelda

"Oh Brian, how could you…and with a workmate!"

Pak (Peter King)

"It's just temporary, until I fix the air conditioner."

Mike Baldwin

"We were convinced there was an Adam Fireplace behind all this plaster and stuff, and we were right – there is!"

Holte (Trevor Holder)

FOOD AND DRINK

Ed McLachlan

"Nice homely atmosphere this place has, Charlie."

Norman Thelwell

Gerard Hoffnung

David Haldane

"It's an old Japanese recipe."

Ed McLachlan

"Which size would you like – mild euphoria, tiresome aggressiveness, maudlin self-pity or lying in the gutter?"

Hector Breeze

"I hope that what he choked on was cooked to his satisfaction."

Frank Cotham

"Don't disturb Sir Roger. He's fermenting."

Michael ffolkes (Brian Davis)

Gerard Hoffnung

"Worked out rather well on the whole...chap next door
wanted a Steinway and I wanted a bar."

Noel Ford

"I can't remember the name but it brought me
out in a warm glow all over."

Michael ffolkes (Brian Davis)

"Oh yes! I've met your sort before."

Holte (Trevor Holder)

"And please hurry. My credit card expires at midnight."

Nick (Nick Hobart)

Tony Reeve

"Of course, every village has got its Global
Village Idiot nowadays."

Neil Bennett

"When you accepted our dinner invitation you implicitly
signed a contract agreeing to eat whatever food
we chose to serve you."

William Haefeli

"Dust and grime, sir?"

Merrily Harpur

"I think I should have warned you –
Brian's not a passive smoker."

Ken Pyne

"You shouldn't drink on an empty life."

Tony Reeve

"I forgot the salt."

George Sprod

"Of course, one can get Italian waiters at home,
but these are fresher."

Merrily Harpur

"Well, well! I'll serve an amusing little white wine!"

Harley Schwadron

"It's a bit rough in here."

Martin Ross

"God! They're bringing a bottle of red again and they know damn well it's going to be fish!"

Chic (Cyril Alfred Jacob)

GARDENING

EricBurgin

"Play 'Raindrops are falling on my conservatory', Stibson."

Holte (Trevor Holder)

"By the way, thanks for looking after the garden
for us while we were on holiday."

Lawrie Siggs

A.F. Wiles

GARDENING

"I understand you've sacked your gardener."

Albert (Albert Rusling)

"I planted Iris this year. Next year I think I'll plant her mother."

Bud Grace

GARDENING

Eric Burgin

Noel Ford

"No! He's my pal."

Charles Barsotti

"Is it too early to prune my climbing hydrangea?"

Bud Grace

"Amazin' stuff! Can't understand why they took it off the market
– I mean, just look at the size of those Brassicas!"

Holte (Trevor Holder)

Ed McLachlan

HEALTH

"Can we get it out, without ruining his suit?"

Simon Bond

HEALTH

Michael Heath

"I suppose I needn't tell *you* the excruciating
agony *this* one's going to give you."

Anton (Beryl Antonia Yeoman)

"Come, come, Mr D'Arcy, I told you
it was going to be a big job."

Roy Raymonde

"Have you tried drink?"

Michael Heath

Ken Pyne

"Don't worry, Mr Bean, we'll soon knock you into shape."

Riana Duncan

"If the Stock Market crashes again –
don't bother trying to revive me."

Geoffrey Dickinson

"Doctor, I get very depressed in between
breakfast, lunch, tea and dinner."

Michael ffolkes (Brian Davis)

"Are you expecting a case of agoraphobia?"

Noel Ford

"…And when did you first become aware
of your intense hatred of children?"

Ajay (Arthur Jackson)

"Mr Pickard! I asked you not to get him too excited!"

Stan McMurtry

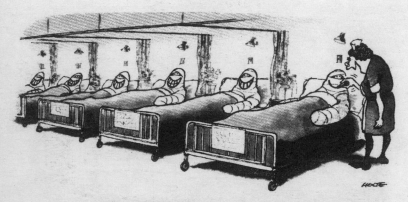

"I know it doesn't make you feel any better, Mr Pendleton,
but it makes my job infinitely more bearable."

Holte (Trevor Holder)

"There's nothing I can do for you – you *are* a duck."

Noel Ford

"Excuse me asking but where did you study dentistry?"

David Myers

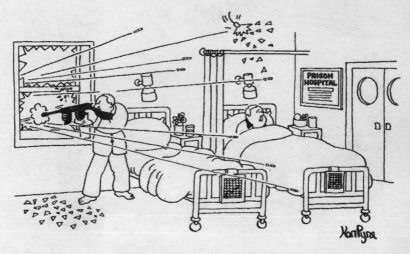

"Nurse! He's out of bed again!"

Ken Pyne

"Relax. He's in a good mood."

Bill Stott

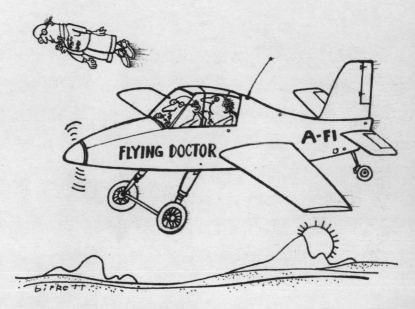

"It's that bloody flying faith-healer again!"

Peter Birkett

HISTORY

Stan McMurtry

"Well, so much for Plan 'A'."

Mike Williams

"Yes, but is there any news of the iceberg?"

Bill Tidy

"Sir Gawain said he was sorry he had slain the woman.
Sir Bors then proposed a resolution opposing the slaying of
women, which was passed. A very large knight rode in and
challenged the entire company; this was tabled for a twelve-
month. There being no further business, we adjourned."

Bud Handelsman

HISTORY

"Aw c'mon, Genghis – we need one more to make up a horde!"

Bill Tidy

"We'd like to appeal against the light."

Mike Williams

"One of the really nice things about the Spring is being able to
turn the central heating down a little."

Mike Williams

HISTORY

"We're not taking this very seriously, are we?"

David Haldane

"We're in deep trouble now – he's begun to have doubts about whether or not he actually is Napoleon."

Ray Lowry

"Just what the hell kind of Viking are you anyhow?"

Mike Williams

"The way they toss their funds around,
they're heading for default!"

Ed Fisher

"The usual mumbo-jumbo about a Pharaoh's curse."

Michael ffolkes (Brian Davis)

"Oh, she **was** a siren once but she's
calmed down a lot since then."

Banx (Jeremy Banks)

"What wine goes with husky?"

Clive Collins

BANX

"They take a pretty hard line with tax evaders here."

Banx (Jeremy Banks)

"Cocktail parties, cocktail parties."

Albert (Albert Rusling)

HOUSES AND
AT HOME

"We'll put it on at £95,000 and hope the athlete's foot
doesn't show on the survey."

Robert Thompson

"It seems we were lulled into a false sense of
security by non-fat frozen yogurt."

William Haefeli

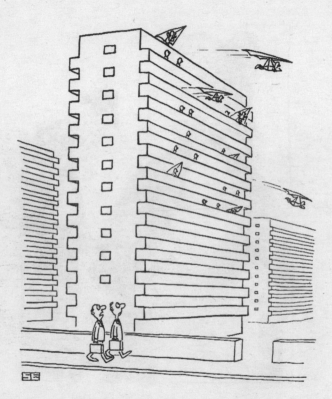

"Looks like number 27's lifts are out of order again."

Stan Eales

"I should decide quickly. It may be gone by tomorrow."

Norman Thelwell

"It's so peaceful, I bet you can hear my car alarm across six valleys."

Robert Thompson

"The market's never been better for the first-time buyer."

Jonathan Pugh

"Are you sure you've been house-hunting before, Tel?"

Robert Thompson

"It's supposed to be automatic, but actually you have to press a button."

Anton (Beryl Antonia Yeoman)

"Good, life is passing the Smith-Watsons by as well."

Nick Baker

André François

"My husband's on nodding acquaintance
with practically every auctioneer in town."

Anton (Beryl Antonia Yeoman)

"The practice of astrology took a major step toward achieving credibility today when, as predicted, everyone born under the sign of Scorpio was run over by an egg lorry."

Bud Grace

"The 4.30 a.m. time check is brought to you by the spirit of mounting personal problems, anxieties and hostile vibes."

Henry Martin

Ed McLachlan

"He'll just lie around, doing nothing, for days now."

Martin Honeysett

"I've been thinking, Harriet. Perhaps I ought to skip the nervous breakdown and go directly into something more serious."

Bud Handelsman

"Oh no, the place has been ransacked!"

David Haldane

"The Pilkingtons! What's the betting the Neighbourhood Watch
Scheme was their idea in the first place!"

Holte (Trevor Holder)

Tony Husband

"Oh, my God! The new neighbours, they've got a telescope!"

Ken Pyne

"Well, gentlemen . . . Shall we join the ladies?"

Stan McMurtry

"It's good for a man to have a hobby."

Holte (Trevor Holder)

"It's the people we were held hostage with that time at the airport.
Do we want to get involved in a reunion dinner?"

William Scully

"They'll be unbearable when they get the swimming pool."

Mike Williams

LONG ARM OF THE LAW

"Fetch me the law for the rich, will you?"

Riana Duncan

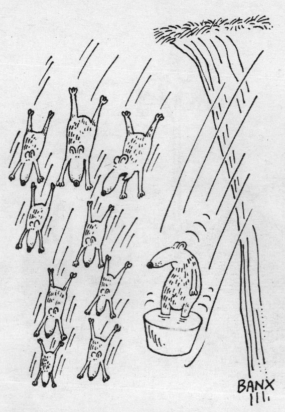

"I suppose it was only a matter of time
before the Mafia muscled in."

Banx (Jeremy Banks)

"I must say, I find the introverts less threatening."

Neil Bennett

"Unfortunately there's no way of knowing whether this is a gang of Teds about to leap on us and kick our teeth in, or a gang of poseurs hanging about waiting for the next trend."

Ray Lowry

"We have reason to believe you are carrying certain substances of a hallucinogenic nature."

Ed McLachlan

"Ernest Pringle, alias Ernie the hypnotist, I sentence you to three months in Barbados, all expenses paid."

David Haldane

"I think the jury has been got at, my lord."

Michael Heath

"Actually, sir, she's out – she leaves the
flag up to fool the burglars."

Noel Ford

"I have your file with me right now, Mr Brown, and I'm rushing
things through as fast as I can."

Martin Honeysett

"Do you seriously expect this court to believe that you witnessed no illegal acts during your eight years on Mr Silver's shoulder?"

Bud Handelsman

"Would you change your name to Chippendale by deed poll, Mr
Hodges? – I have a sudden twinge of conscience."

Anton (Beryl Antonia Yeoman)

Client (to solicitor). "So I said to them,
'I've tried to get a settlement by fair means and failed.
You will now hear from my lawyer.'"

D. L. Ghilchik

"I'm afraid I can't help you; civil liberties are outside my domain. I specialize in jungle law."

Bud Handelsman

LONG ARM OF THE LAW

"It's clues we're looking for, constable."

Martin Honeysett

"Nothing personal, Mr Knight, but I was hoping
to speak to one of the others."

Tony Husband

"Then, of course, there'll be the usual search fee."

Norman Thelwell

"I'm terribly sorry – I can't understand
a single word you're saying."

Ed McLachlan

"Somehow I don't think we'll ever know the whole story."

Michael ffolkes (Brian Davis)

"Yes, O High One, one previous conviction."

Clive Collins

"Bank of England...Inquiries? As a matter of interest, I should like to know whether Mr O'Brien, the new Chief Cashier, spells his name with an apostrophe."

Anton (Beryl Antonia Yeoman)

MEDIA

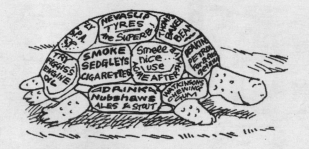

"The authorities have denied permission to film the actual street fighting. I have, however, obtained clearance to show you my room at the Hilton, and here it is."

Bud Handelsman

Clive Goddard

NEWSPAPERS

MAGAZINES

THROWAWAY-LINES

BROKEN DREAMS

Mike Williams

"Now can we have it as a sound bite?"

Joel Mishon

"Yes, I admit it's interesting, but please remember WE've been sent out to record the first cuckoo."

Anton (Beryl Antonia Yeoman)

"Sire, the peasants are rebelling against product placement."

Jim Sizemore

Les Barton

"So, please, dig a little deeper and help us get rid of pop-up ads for good."

Mike Baldwin

"He's come up with a damn fine product there – but his presentation's bloody awful."

Ray Lowry

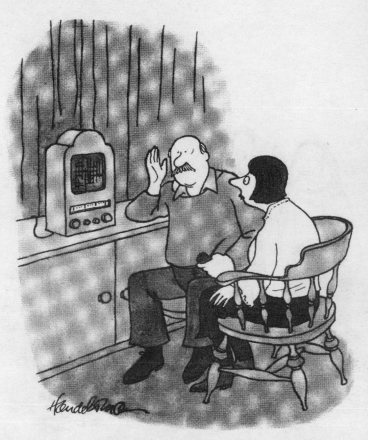

"This is the voice of Moderation. I wouldn't go so far as to say we have actually **seized** the radio station."

Bud Handelsman

"Wayne's into advertising."

Clive Goddard

"He always wins, but I earn more from advertising."

Nick Baker

MUSIC AND ENTERTAINMENT

MUSIC AND
ENTERTAINMENT

"It's been a truly harrowing experience. It was almost impossible to combine the right degree of reverence with my nauseating stream of trivial, mindless chit-chat."

Ray Lowry

Steve Way

"This next song relates to my struggle to come to terms with a
receding hairline at age twenty-five."

Ray Lowry

"Came home this morning, found my best gal messin' roun'. Came home this morning, found my best gal messin' roun'. Took out that twelve-gauge shotgun, and done blown that woman down."

Peter Birkett

"The Man in Black? Are you trying to
tell me you're Johnny Cash?"

Ray Lowry

"Seems like nothing'll cheer him up."

Bill Tidy

"Poor Henry misses so much, being deaf."

Kenneth Mahood

"What I really miss is that huge ball of fluff that used to accumulate on the stylus…"

Ray Lowry

"I've forgotten which tune we're improvising on."

Eric Burgin

"Jazz is back!"

Michael Heath

"Remember, this is an important interview – I'll do the talking."

Peter Birkett

"He sold out years ago."

Michael Heath

"He was okay with the sex and drugs.
It was the rock 'n' roll that finished him."

Tony Husband

"Now just play as you like to play on
your own – forget the mikes."

Michael Heath

"But we just saw all of them at the Save the Trees concert."

William Haefeli

"Are you sure tonight was bingo night?"

Michael Heath

"I'm under doctor's orders to mime my screams."

J.W. Taylor

"I joined a pop group because I was sick of standing around tending a piece of soulless office equipment all day."

Ray Lowry

Harley Schwadron

"Bad news, I'm afraid. Our artistic licence has expired!"

Ray Lowry

PARTIES

"Good Lord, you mustn't believe everything
you read in the papers about journalists."

Banx (Jeremy Banks)

"Let me see if we have an extra large in a pumpkin."

Mike Twohy

"Amanda tells me you cook. I eat."

Sewell (Patricia Carter)

"Frank is into unofficial strike action…
Harry is into working to rule…Bob is into picketing…
and Walter here is into impotent rage."

Kenneth Mahood

"Hey, let's not underestimate science! I bet they're working on a replacement to the ozone layer right now."

Bud Handelsman

"Would you mind if you passively smoked?"

Matt (Matthew Pritchett)

"This is the worst hen party I've ever been to."

Robert Thompson

"Melville's an economist. In his predictions he's been right just once in a hundred, enough to give him a considerable reputation."

William Scully

"At a party, Irwin, why do you insist on labelling everyone?"

Harley Schwadron

"Oh, how embarrassing, there's a woman
over there wearing the same cosmetic surgery."

Martin Ross

"For heaven's sake, Brian! Can't you forget for one
minute that you're a chartered surveyor?"

Ken Pyne

"I'm desperate for a cause."

Tony Husband

"Ignore Harold, he only does it to get attention."

Neil Bennett

"Well, here we are with our personal computer, ready for any
twists and turns the conversation may take."

Bud Handelsman

"I'm 10 per cent lover, 8 per cent poet and 2 per cent head librarian. The rest, I'm afraid, is water."

John Donegan

POLITICS

"Have you got any that *aren't* flame retardant?"

Clive Goddard

"You'll like this one. It performs a thousand revolutions a minute."

Naf (Andy McKay)

"It says here that the government are in danger of squandering the Conservatives' Golden Economic Legacy."

Clive Goddard

"No you idiot! They're supposed to throw eggs at us!"

Adey Bryant

Clive Goddard

"Fidel – do you have next month's election results?"

Deacon (Dave Connaughton)

Clive Goddard

"Thank God you've come, officer. This lunatic wants to know where Downing Street is so he can assassinate our beloved Prime Minister."

"Right, sir…you go down Palmer Street, turn right at Tothill Street, first left at Queen Anne's Gate."

Ed McLachlan

The Asylum Seekers.

Clive Goddard

Western Powers make their contribution to resolving
environmental issues.

Fran Orford

RELATIONSHIPS AND SEX

"Linda and I are getting a divorce,
and we divided up our friends. I got you."

Charles Saxon

"Neville agreed to settle out of court."

Albert (Albert Rusling)

"I don't know why I don't leave you."

Anton (Beryl Antonia Yeoman)

"I've won ten days in Paris with the companion of my choice."

J.W. Taylor

"Any other man would have built a raft."

Michael ffolkes (Brian Davis)

"We've been married twenty-five years, Helen.
You could at least give me a chance to run for it."

Frank Cotham

"Leave me if you must, Marjorie, but to run away with my best friend, that's what really hurts."

Riana Duncan

"Gerald, I don't think our both being left-handed is enough."

Michael ffolkes (Brian Davis)

"Frankly, what attracted me to Sylvia in the first place
was the prospect of some really kinky sex. Of course, that was
replaced with a deep and abiding mutual love."

Bud Grace

"When we first met he was tremendously rampant."

Michael ffolkes (Brian Davis)

"He's a lousy provider but, boy, can he *kiss*."

Noel Ford

"I grew up in a dysfunctional family. Of course, no one used that term back then so we thought we were normal."

William Haefeli

"Marvin still has plenty of virility, although of course these days most of it goes into real estate."

Bud Handelsman

"What a day! Round in seventy-five and now this."

Alex Graham

"OK, so I'm not the man you thought I was.
Is it my fault you're a lousy judge of character?"

William Haefeli

"Other women? What other women?"

David Haldane

"No doubt you've heard of my reputation as a bit of a man-eater."

Tony Husband

"I'm sorry – what's your name again? When you told me I'd no reason to believe I'd want to remember."

William Haefeli

"But you *can't* expect me to stick to my New Year's resolution to give up booze. I was drunk when I made it."

Riana Duncan

"There are still some things to sort out."

Ed Fisher

"My family's all grown up now – except my husband, of course."

John Donegan

"Couldn't you at least wait until half-time so
we could discuss our communication problem?"

Harley Schwadron

"I'm sorry about The Seventh Wonder of the World Award,
darling. They've given it to a lighthouse."

Michael ffolkes (Brian Davis)

"I'm not afraid of commitment. I'm afraid of you."

William Haefeli

"Your accountant will have explained the difference between tax evasion and tax avoidance – well, the same principle applies to birth control."

Merrily Harpur

"Mmm, I just love to run my fingers through a man's wallet."

Ed McLachlan

"One look at you and I said, 'Now here's a guy who's not going to fool around with silly opening one-liners.'"

Harley Schwadron

"Oh, it was you. I thought it was a mosquito whining."

Riana Duncan

RELIGION

"Hear the chain squeaking? I tell you he's on a bike."

David Myers

"My father wanted me to go into his insurance business and I
wanted to go into the theatre, so we compromised."

Ken Pyne

"Seven Deadly Sins are enough. We're dumping Incompetence."

Michael ffolkes (Brian Davis)

"I'm sorry, but you've got to have at least two As and a B."

Nick Newman

"You're being reincarnated as a mayfly,
Mr Hoskins – have a nice day."

Banx (Jeremy Banks)

"Don't take any notice of them –
they're doing a series for the BBC."

Michael Heath

"Mind you, I had hoped to have met a
few more famous dead people by now."

Riana Duncan

"There must be more to the After-life than
hanging around the British Museum."

Peter Birkett

"There's usually four of us but Pestilence
is running in the 3.30 at Uttoxeter."

Banx (Jeremy Banks)

"Congratulations! What got you here is your total lack of
commitment to any ideology."

Harley Schwadron

SCHOOLS AND UNIVERSITY

ffolkes

"Congratulations class! Apart from one, you all passed the
humanitarian rights exam."

Naf (Andy McKay)

"En français, Jackson, en français."

J.W. Taylor

"Very well, Geoffrey – you have received fair warning.
I am going to confiscate your brick."

Hector Breeze

"Smirking or Non-Smirking?"

Clive Goddard

"Fortunately for him he has the best left hook in the school."

Michael ffolkes (Brian Davis)

"Now sir, you say the vandals got in last night and wrecked the classrooms but no-one noticed until about 11.45 this morning."

Ed McLachlan

"About these experiments of yours into genetic cloning, Bond,"
boomed the Headmaster. "They must cease immediately."

Bruce Baillie

"They've told me to stand outside until
they feel like behaving themselves."

Martin Honeysett

Clive Goddard

Ed McLachlan

Neil Bennett

"We've got a few left over, folks – who wants 'em?"

Bud Grace

SCIENCE

"Naturally, when I volunteered to become a guinea-pig,
it never occurred to me…"

Noel Ford

"This is the afterlife?"

Banx (Jeremy Banks)

"Never mind what's wrong with 'im –
just read the meter and go."

Holte (Trevor Holder)

"What's amazing is no two cats or dogs are alike!"

Eli (Eli Bauer)

Mike Williams

"Well done, Haskett – the research grant is yours."

Noel Ford

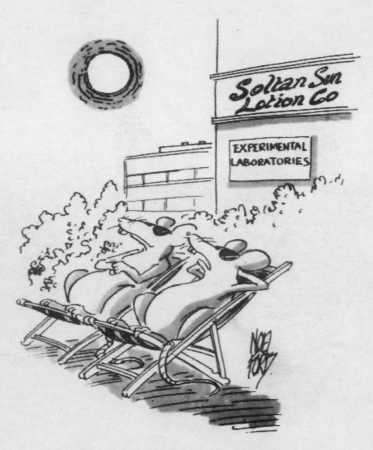

"Bit of luck, that – landing a cushy summer job."

Noel Ford

George Sprod

"I still say there's got to be a catch somewhere."

Banx (Jeremy Banks)

"Yes?"

Mike Williams

SHOPPING

"Will you be paying by cheque, credit card,
money, or are you shoplifting?"

Michael Heath

"Whoops, must get that laser fixed."

Martin Ross

"I'll have the avocado shampoo accompanied by the egg
conditioner, with the oyster and cider vinegar cleansing milk to
follow, and perhaps just a tiny pot of peach and strawberry hand
cream to finish off with . . ."

Merrily Harpur

"It's got more special-function keys than you'll find on many of the larger models: square root, cosine, logarithmic, integral and exponential keys. I'd say that more than makes up for the fact that it doesn't have the number nine!"

Ed Fisher

"I'll take them!"

Eli (Eli Bauer)

SHOPPING

ONE
SIZE
NOT YOU

Steve Way

SPACE AND ALIENS

"All right – if this is the way you want it. But don't forget we came here with peaceful intentions."

Leslie Starke

Ed Fisher

"Doesn't it make you sick? Our baggage has been sent to Jupiter."

Nick (Nick Hobart)

"It's a damn sight better than the weather we've been having lately, I can tell you."

Holte (Trevor Holder)

SPORT

"You mean we **all** think badminton's a bloody boring game and
we'd **all** prefer to spend our evenings in the pub?"

Ken Pyne

"I keep telling you, Mr Olmroyd – an injury resulting
from a late tackle in the 1914 Christmas Day football
match does **not** qualify as a war wound."

Peter Birkett

"I see the Hitachi deal fell through."

Albert (Albert Rushling)

"That'll do for today's lesson."

Unknown

"I think we could pacify them if we could persuade
our members to cook and eat the fox afterwards."

Bernard Cookson

SPORT

Tombs (M.F. Tombs)

"Bit of a rough game today I'm afraid, Mrs Titmarsh."

Martin Honeysett

"Do you think there's somewhere up there
where they don't play football?"

Michael Heath

"My God, McGregor, what do you mean – it's only a game?"

Michael ffolkes (Brian Davis)

Harley Schwadron

"It's remarkable how she still keeps
coming back year after year…"

Nick Newman

"Now what?"

Bud Grace

Eli (Eli Bauer)

"Mind if we play through, old man?
My bleeper's been going since the 14th."

Noel Ford

"Whoever you are, this is your lucky day. The ball hit you just as
a doctor and a lawyer happened to be passing."

Bud Handelsman

"Come on down, we're all in the bar!"

Bruce Leslie Petty

"Oh God – not **another** moral victory."

J.W. Taylor

TRAVEL AND MOTORING

"Listen, pal, if you're not entirely satisfied, bring it back and we'll put another one over on you."

Henry Martin

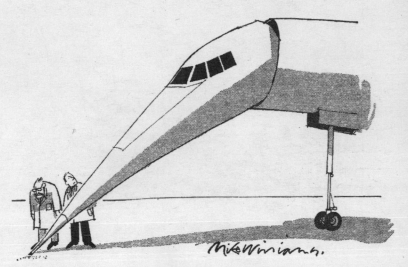

"You're right! It is eating ants."

Mike Williams

"Oh, darling! It's just like the brochure."

Michael Heath

"I don't believe it's been touched! Where are the reassuring oily finger marks on the steering wheel, the greasy smears on the upholstery, the smudges on the paintwork, the footprints on the carpet?"

Leslie Starke

"Squatters!"

David Myers

Steve Way

"Parkinson! For heaven's sake, man, stop or we'll all be killed!"

Mike Williams

"Holy recession, Batman. It's not the same
since we lost our company car."

David Haldane

David Langdon

"I could only afford the one week!"

Albert (Albert Rusling)

"Let's get moving. I'm beginning to feel
like an advert for a pension fund."

William Scully

Pete Dredge

THE BRITISH CHARACTER
LOVE OF TRAVELLING ALONE

Pont (Graham Laidler)

Matt (Matthew Pritchett)

"Just because we are English you needn't think my sister
and I won't make a fuss about this."

Pont (Graham Laidler)

"How can I be sure the money will reach the snake?"

Banx (Jeremy Banks)

Stan Eales

Banx (Jeremy Banks)

"Personally, I wouldn't recommend Spain."

Bestie (Steve Best)

"Look, if it upsets you so much, Harry…"

Bernard Cookson

Tony Husband

"Of course, some of the sense of wonder and mystery disappears when you find that it's the local McDonald's."

Alan de la Nougerede

"Oh, I'd say it's about ten minutes to three."

Bud Grace

"I'm afraid you'll have to stop the bus –
Mrs Scully needs the lavatory again."

David Haldane

"This is your Captain speaking… I apologize for the
bumpy ride. We are now flying at about ten feet…
Mr Tatlow's had a go… who's next?"

Holte (Trevor Holder)

"We went round the world last year but didn't like it."

David Hawker

"Another thing about Liechtenstein – their road maps are really easy to fold."

Nick (Nick Hobart)

"Skimped a bit on the lifeboats, haven't they."

David Myers

"OK, everyone's gone – you can pick it up now."

Nick (Nick Hobart)

"You know, it's nice to go travelling but it's
oh so nice to come home."

Tony Husband

Nick (Nick Hobart)

"The trouble these days is that the jet-set is full of the people that I originally joined the jet-set to get away from!"

Ken Pyne

WAR

"We're not fighting, mum, we're playing peace talks."

Clive Goddard

"Secretly trained by the Americans? That's funny, so were we."

Ed Fisher

"Now's a good time to get a feel for your negotiating skills."

Andrew Toos

Private Teale had mild reservations about the
newly designed army gear.

Chris Bray-Cotton

"I'm in a chat room with one of the guys in the castle…
he's really quite nice."

Andrew Toos

"Sergeant – I'm going over the top…"

Ham Khan

Harvey supports the right to bare arms.

Myke Ashley-Cooper

"Well, that's buggered that idea."

Mike Mosedale

"We must be on a stealth mission: he's using brushes."

Philip Berkin

"Do the M.O.D. let many of their staff work at home?"

Richard Jolley

CARTOONISTS' BIOGRAPHIES

Ajay (Arthur Jackson) b. 1912 Started work as a junior artist in a company making cinema signs before spending 18 months as a ladies' underwear salesman. He sold his first cartoon to a British national daily at the age of 15 and went on to draw for children's comics such as *Beano*, *Dandy* and *Topper*. He also painted portraits, including one of George Bernard Shaw, which the playwright owned.

Albert (Albert Rusling) b. 1944 A native of Liverpool who left school at 15 to work in an advertising agency. Self-taught as an artist, he became a full-time cartoonist from 1968 and went on to illustrate a number of books as well as drawing the *Private Eye* strip "Old Macdonald".

Anton (Beryl Antonia Yeoman) 1907–70 The daughter of a rancher, she was born in Australia before sailing with her family to England at the age of four. As a teenager she lost two fingers of her right hand, subsequently learning to write and draw with her left. At first the signature "Anton" was a joint venture between Beryl and her brother Harold but from 1949 she took sole control. "I was quite modern when I started," she recalled. "I was told a couple of bishops had given up *Punch* when I started drawing for them." Her skill at being able to capture all levels of society – from spivs and forgers to dukes and duchesses – found a ready outlet for her work in such varied markets as *Tatler* and *Men Only*.

Artz, Sally b. 1935 Has worked for *Reader's Digest*, *Punch*, *Private Eye* and the *Spectator*, producing topical press cartoons as well as long-running strips. Among the many children's books she has illustrated was *Sex Ed* by Dr Miriam Stoppard. Lives in Bath, England.

Ashley-Cooper, Myke b. 1941 He runs a website for cartoonists in his native South Africa and has drawn regularly for South Africa's top investigative monthly magazine, *Noseweek*. He specializes in pun and cliché single gag cartoons.

Baillie, Bruce b. 1955 A prolific greetings card artist, he was first published in 1975 and has since worked for many UK card companies, including Hanson White, Wharps and Britannia. He trained for four years at Batley Art College in Yorkshire and has also illustrated a number of children's books.

Baker, Nick b. 1940 A graduate of Ealing Art School, London, his first cartoon was published in the *Evening Standard* in 1966. His work has subsequently appeared in the likes of *Private Eye*, the *Spectator*, the *Financial Times*, *Sunday Telegraph* and *Mail on Sunday* and he has also illustrated a number of books.

Baldwin, Mike b. 1954 Since having his first cartoon published in his local paper, *The Burlington, Ontario Gazette*, in 1976, Baldwin has seen his work appear in hundreds of newspapers across Canada and the US, principally via his syndicated cartoon "Cornered". He has illustrated a number of academic textbooks, specializing in off-beat humour in the form of single panel colour gags.

Banx (Jeremy Banks) b. 1959 After studying at Maidstone College of Art, Banx drew his first series in the 1980s – "Mister Bignose" in the anarchic children's comic *Oink!* He has since supplied cartoons to the

BIOGRAPHIES

Financial Times, Evening Standard and many others. He took on the animal strip "Cecil" for the *Daily Express* and has also worked in the field of animation on the mini-series *The Many Deaths of Norman Spittal.*

Barsotti, Charles b. 1933 Texan illustrator who was cartoon editor of the *Saturday Evening Post* until it folded in 1969. The following year he began a long association with the *New Yorker.* He wrote and drew a strip, "Sally Bananas", from the late 1960s and received the National Cartoonist Society Gag Cartoon Award in 1988. His rounded, elegant, sparsely detailed style evokes both the traditional world of a James Thurber and the contemporary sensibility of a Roz Chast.

Barton, Les b. 1923 A former telegraph clerk and commercial artist, Dorset-born Barton made his name in children's comics. Signing his early work "Lezz", he was a regular contributor to *Punch* from 1954. During the Falklands War in 1982 he was staff war artist on the *Sun.*

Bennett, Neil b. 1941 Born in Warsop, Nottinghamshire, his first cartoon was published in 1960. However he spent 23 years as an English teacher before becoming a full-time cartoonist at the age of 46. He uses fibre tip pens on bank paper.

Berkin, Philip b. 1959 He worked as a steel erector, a surveyor and a farm worker before taking up cartooning. Berkin's work has been published in *Private Eye*, the *Spectator, Punch* and many others. Lives in London.

Bestie (Steve Best) b. 1954 Since studying Fine Art at Bristol, he has designed countless cartoons and greeting cards. In 1987 he provided cartoons for the short-lived *News on Sunday* and nine years later published a selection of his work under the title *All the Bestie.* In 2002 he helped design the musical *DANGER – Vacuum!* at the Williamson Art Gallery, Birkenhead.

Birkett, Peter Often described as the cartoonists' favourite cartoonist, Birkett was a *Punch* favourite in the early 1980s even though his output was relatively low. However his classic Daleks' cartoon became popular around the world. Birkett's drawings are characterized by precise yet fluid line work, his quirky, frequently black, gags and his familiar squat figures.

Bond, Simon b. 1947 A diplomat's son, he was born in New York but studied art in England. Worked as a paste-up artist on *Tatler* and as manager of a jewellery shop before returning to the US where he contributed cartoons to the likes of *National Lampoon* and the *New Yorker*. Settling back in England in the early 1980s, he has penned a series of best-selling books, including *101 Uses for a Dead Cat, How To Thrive on Rejection, Unspeakable Acts, Uses of a Dead Cat in History,* and *Battered Lawyers and Other Good Ideas.*

Bray-Cotton, Chris b. 1962 An Australian cartoonist who sold his first work to *Good Weekend* magazine in 1992. He has staged an exhibition in Melbourne called "Hysterical Women" and illustrated the book *DIY Feminism.*

Breeze, Hector b. 1928 London-born Hector Breeze studied art at evening classes while working in a government drawing office and sold his first cartoon to *Melody Maker* in 1957. He has since produced cartoons for a wide range of publications and became the Pocket Cartoonist on the *Daily Express* in 1982. He is best known for his drawings of impoverished gentry with characteristic chinless faces and tiny dot eyes. Ralph Steadman wrote in 1996 that Breeze's "clumsy bewildered characters restore my faith in the seriously daft".

BIOGRAPHIES

Brown, David b. 1932 First published in *Cosmopolitan* in 1967, the Canada-based cartoonist has had his work featured in magazines and newspapers worldwide. He has also served as animation director on around 100 films. Winner of a Silver Medal at the Chicago Film Fest in 1982, he has illustrated and written a number of books, including *Girls of Washington*, *About Antiques* and *Court Jesters Cartoons*.

Bryant, Adey Since selling his first cartoon to the *Sun*, he has built up a wide portfolio of clients, including *Private Eye*, *News of the World*, *Daily Mirror*, *Fiesta*, and assorted football fanzines and greeting card companies. He recently illustrated a book, *Bad Christmas*, about people's festive mishaps. Born in Portsmouth, he currently lives in Huntingdon.

Burgin, Eric 1926–66 Educated in Maidenhead, Berkshire, Burgin began drawing cartoons in 1945 whilst serving with the RAF in Singapore. He became a full-time freelance cartoonist in 1954, producing a series of illustrated anagrams called "Anagrins" for the *Evening News* and a series called "The Nitelys", about a family of television fanatics, for the *Daily Sketch*. His cartoons depicted a suburban lifestyle that was instantly recognizable and he was voted the Cartoonists' Club of Great Britain Humorous Cartoonist of the Year three times – in 1962, 1963 and 1964. Died of a heart attack aged 40.

Chic (Cyril Alfred Jacob) 1926–2000 Born in Dulwich, London, he claimed that most of his education was acquired as an evacuee to the Sussex countryside during the Second World War. After serving in the Royal Navy in south-east Asia, a spell in farming and the circulation department of the *Daily Express*, he became a freelance cartoonist in 1963. He was also a scriptwriter for radio and television.

BIOGRAPHIES

Cheney, Tom b. 1954 Born in Norfolk, Virginia, his work has appeared in over 500 publications, including *National Lampoon, Penthouse,* and the *Wall Street Journal.* In 1985 he won the Scripps-Howard Outstanding Cartoonist Award. He lives in Hawaii and is currently a staff cartoonist for the *New Yorker* and a contributing artist and writer for *MAD Magazine.*

Collins, Clive b. 1942 After working in marine insurance and as a film extra, he became political cartoonist on the *Sun* in 1969. A year later he was appointed the first political cartoonist on the *People,* signing himself "Collie". He also stood in for Jak on the *Evening Standard* and adopted the pseudonym "Ollie" for his *Standard* work during the Falklands War. Voted Cartoonist of the Year by the Cartoonists' Club of Great Britain in 1984, 1985 and 1987.

Cookson, Bernard b. 1937 The son of an engineer, Cookson attended Manchester Art School and worked in an advertising agency before making his mark as a cartoonist. In 1966 he took over the *Daily Sketch* strip "The Nitelys" from the late Eric Burgin and from 1969 until 1976 was social/political cartoonist on the *Evening News.* In 1982 he replaced Clive Collins as Franklin's deputy on the *Sun* and four years later became Griffin's deputy on the *Express.* He draws with a Pentel pen on cartridge paper.

Cotham, Frank Worked in graphics at a Memphis TV station for 13 years, doing cartoons in his spare time. He took two years to make his first sale – to *Saturday Review* – but since concentrating on cartooning as a full-time career his work has appeared in such prestigious publications as the *New Yorker.* He says: "I think an aspiring cartoonist should understand that making money in this business is a long shot at best."

BIOGRAPHIES

Davis, Roy 1921–2004 Having been told by his headmaster that one day he would be published in *Punch*, Davis's first job was as a general studio artist with London wallpaper designers Arthur Sanderson and Sons. While working for them in 1939, he had his first cartoon published in the weekly magazine *Answers*. After the war he joined Gaumont British Animation as a storyman, helping to devise scripts for animated films. In 1950 he became a full-time cartoonist, specializing in captionless cartoons. He wrote over 10,000 stories for children's magazines and was still working well into his seventies.

De la Nougerede, Alan b. 1932 After studying oil painting with St John Earp and Cynthia Weller, he had his first cartoon published in the *Evening Standard*. He has since supplied material for the likes of *Penthouse*, *Esquire*, *Mayfair*, *Punch*, *Private Eye*, *Sunday People*, *Weekend* and the *Daily Mirror*. He did the strips "Brit" and "Napoleon" for the *Express* and *Evening News* respectively. Lives in Surrey.

Deacon (Dave Connaughton) b. 1940 He has come a long way since having his first professional drawing published on a pet food can at the age of 15. He has gone on to sell cartoons all over the world and has won awards at a number of international cartoon competitions. Based in Worcester, England, he specializes in gag cartoons.

Dickinson, Geoffrey 1933–88 Liverpool-born cartoonist who originally intended to be a landscape painter. After freelancing for the BBC graphics department, he became deputy art editor of *Punch* in 1967 and produced many covers for the magazine. *Time* magazine chose him to do the cover for its "Swinging London" issue in 1966.

BIOGRAPHIES

Donegan, John b. 1926 Londoner Donegan worked as an art director for an advertising agency before becoming a full-time cartoonist in 1975. Famous for his dog cartoons, which have been compiled in a number of books, he won the Designers and Art Directors Award in 1964 for his posters for the *Sunday Times*.

Dredge, Pete b. 1952 Raised in Nottingham, Dredge worked as a graphic designer before submitting a collection of cartoons to *Punch* in 1976. To his delight and amazement, they accepted three straight away. One of the first he sold was of two seedy, dishevelled-looking blokes walking down the road, and one saying to the other: "Don't look now but your flies are done up!" By 1980 he had tasted the success of his first *Punch* cover and was writing sketches for the BBC TV comedy series *Not the Nine O'Clock News*. He has also had work published by *National Lampoon*, *Men Only*, *Mayfair*, *Private Eye*, *Penthouse* and *Radio Times*.

Duncan, Riana b. 1950 Although born in Paisley, Scotland, Duncan is half Dutch and studied graphics at the Free Academy of Fine Arts in The Hague. Apart from her cartooning, she has written and illustrated a number of children's books. Her homes have included a 35-foot yacht and a windmill in France.

Eales, Stan b. 1962 Having trained in graphic design, New Zealander Eales had his first cartoon published in the *Auckland Star* in 1983. Now based in England, his work has appeared in *Punch*, *Private Eye* and the *Spectator* and he has also illustrated four cartoon books, including *Isn't Progress Wonderful?*

Eli (Eli Bauer) d. 1998 Bauer was a magazine and comic-book cartoonist in the US for DC Comics, *Collier's*, *National Lampoon*,

Playboy and many others. He worked as a storyman and layout designer for Ray Patin Productions and Terrytoons, for whom he created the character Hector Heathcote. He formed a production company with Al Kouzel that created *Sesame Street* spots, commercials and the TV series *Winky Dink and You.*

ffolkes, Michael (Brian Davis) 1925–88 The son of a commercial graphic artist, he sold his first drawing to *Punch* at the age of 17, signing it "brian." Following the war, he studied painting at Chelsea School of Art and adopted the name "Michael ffolkes" after thumbing through a copy of *Burke's Peerage.* In 1955 he began illustrating Michael Wharton's "Way of the World" column in the *Daily Telegraph* and from 1961 illustrated the film reviews in *Punch.* A flamboyant character, ffolkes specialized in mythological and historical cartoons, frequently adorned with large sexy ladies. Indeed he claimed to be the first person to draw "sexually desirable women" in *Punch.*

Fisher, Ed b. 1926 Born in New York City, Fisher contributed cartoons to *Punch* and the *New Yorker* from the early 1950s. He has won a number of awards and has compiled five books of cartoons, including *Ed Fisher's Doomsday Book, Maestro Please* and *The Animal Songbook.*

Ford, Noel b. 1942 Ford enjoyed a variety of careers – furniture salesman, laboratory technician, guitarist in a rock band – before turning to cartooning. First published in his local paper, the *Nuneaton Evening Tribune,* he went on to become deputy editorial cartoonist to Bill Caldwell on the *Daily Star* and has been editorial cartoonist on the *Church Times* since 1989. He has provided more than 30 cover illustrations for *Punch* and has worked in advertising for such companies as Thomas Cook, Guinness and British Telecom.

BIOGRAPHIES

François, André (André Farkas) 1915–2005 Born to a Jewish family in Romania, he became a French citizen in 1939. He worked as a painter, sculptor and graphic designer, but is best remembered for his cartoons, whose subtle humour bear comparison to those of Saul Steinberg. François worked initially for French left-wing newspapers but gradually reached a wider audience, publishing in *Punch* and the *New Yorker*.

Ghilchik, D.L. 1892–1972 David Louis Ghilchik was born in Romania and came to England at the age of five. His father wanted him to take up medicine but young David won a place at Manchester School of Art where his contemporary students included L.S. Lowry. Between the wars he contributed largely social and domestic jokes to *Punch* before becoming a political cartoonist on the *Daily Sketch* during the Second World War.

Gilligan b. 1954 A regular contributor to *The Wall Street Journal, Chicago Tribune, Washington Times* and many others, Gilligan has also illustrated over thirty children's books. A graduate of the University of British Columbia, he has staged exhibitions in and around Toronto and won an award from the Canadian Marketing Association. His whimsical and intelligent wit has been applied to everything from selling products to adding much-needed humour to dry financial reports.

Goddard, Clive b. 1960 A trained graphic designer, Oxford-based Goddard sold his first cartoon to *Private Eye* in 1996 and has since featured in *Punch, The New Statesman, The Oldie, Spectator, The Times, Reader's Digest,* and many more. He has also illustrated various Scholastic books for children, including the "Dead Famous" series.

Grace, Bud b. 1952 Born in Chester, Pennsylvania, Grace moved to Florida with his family when he was five years old. There, he earned a doctorate in physics and published articles on a variety of scientific topics, including low-energy neutron scattering. In 1979, with no previous experience, he suddenly decided to draw and sold his work to major magazines before creating the successful comic strip *Piranha Club Ernie*.

Graham, Alex 1917–91 Scottish cartoonist Alex Graham had been drawing "Wee Hughie" in the *Dundee Weekly News* for 18 years before his most famous creation – "Fred Basset" – was launched in the *Daily Mail* in 1963. The dog was said to have been inspired by Graham's own basset hound, Freida. Graham also drew the "Graham's Golf Club" series of cartoons for *Punch* and, in the view of William Hewison, "has probably got more mileage out of the cocktail party than any other cartoonist."

Grizelda, Based in Hove, Sussex, Grizelda is one of Britain's leading female cartoonists. Her work has appeared in *Private Eye*, the *Spectator, Big Issue, the Oldie, Diva,* and *Red Pepper* and she has illustrated the books *Dumb Britain* and *MediaBalls*.

Haefeli, William After working in a Chicago advertising agency, Haefeli ventured into cartooning, becoming a regular contributor to *Punch* and the *New Yorker*. Comparing the two countries' sense of humour, he says: "In England you don't have to make a terribly original observation, but if you say it in a funny way, they'll appreciate it. Americans think that something said cleverly means the person is trying too hard." Haefeli's cartoons are typically clean and spare. "I only draw as much as is necessary for the joke. It's the joke first and then the composition. If you look at my drawings, all my characters look really similar. It's their expressions that change."

Hagen, Ralph b. 1959 Self-taught with a little help from the Alberta College of Art, Hagen sold his first cartoon to the *Stony Plain Reporter* in 1976. Since then his work has appeared in such diverse publications as *Reader's Digest*, *Diver Magazine* and *Worksite News*. He has also illustrated high school maths textbooks for Canadian students.

Haldane, David b. 1954 In addition to his work as a joke and strip cartoonist, Haldane, who was born in Blyth, Northumberland, wrote scripts for the satirical TV series *Spitting Image*. His cartoons have appeared in *Punch*, the *Guardian*, *Sunday Times* and the *Observer* and he has also worked on advertising campaigns for the supermarket chain Asda and Pedigree Chum dog food as well as designing greeting cards for Camden Graphics.

Handelsman, Bud b. 1922 Bernard "Bud" Handelsman was born in New York City, serving in the US Army during the Second World War. In 1963 he moved to England and spent almost 20 years there before returning to the US. He contributed the "Freaky Fables" series for Punch and his work has also appeared in the *New Statesman*, the *New Yorker*, *Esquire* and *Playboy*, for whom he won Best Black and White Cartoon Award in 1978. His animated film *In the Beginning* was shown on BBC television in 1992.

Harpur, Merrily b. 1948 Educated at Oxford and Dublin, Harpur restored oil paintings before becoming a freelance cartoonist. She contributed "Merrily Harpur's Diary" and the strip "Flavia Corkscrew's Good Food Guide" to *The Times* and the series "Chattering Classes" and the strip "The Arcadians" to the *Sunday Telegraph*. She also produced animated titles and cartoon backdrops for Miles Kington's TV series *Let's Parler Franglais*.

Harris, Sidney Harris was born in Brooklyn and attended the Art Students League in New York. In 1955 he began his career as a science cartoonist and has since drawn thousands of cartoons on the subject, which have appeared in such publications as *American Scientist, Physics Today, New Yorker* and *National Lampoon*.

Hawker, David b. 1941 Has worked in such diverse jobs as a salesman, gardener, laundry assistant and driving instructor. Self-taught, he sold his first cartoon in 1967 while working as an agricultural draughtsman. He went full-time as a freelance cartoonist two years later and has sold to the likes of *Punch*, the *Spectator* and *Private Eye*.

Heath, Michael b. 1935 After studying at Brighton College of Art, he worked as an animator at Rank before becoming a cartoonist in 1956. His work has since appeared in numerous publications and he is currently cartoon editor of the *Spectator*. He has an acute eye for the changing fads and fashions of urban life. Heath always uses a dip pen and India ink – never uses pencil.

Hewison, William 1925–2002 Born in South Shields, Durham, he studied painting in London and taught art part-time while developing a freelance career in graphics. He became a regular contributor to *Punch*, joining the magazine's editorial staff in 1957 and becoming its art editor three years later. He left the art editorship in 1984 to return to freelancing.

Hoffnung, Gerard 1925–59 Born in Berlin (he came to London in 1939 as a schoolboy refugee), Hoffnung was an accomplished musician and artist and is remembered for his cartoons that poked gentle fun at conductors and orchestra members. Any inanimate object he drew seemed to take on a personality of its own. "I would try to draw something," he once said, "a chair for instance, and there it would be – with an expression. I had almost nothing to do with it."

Holland, Tony b. 1932 Taught English, history and maths at schools in Leicestershire and London before becoming a professional cartoonist and illustrator. He sold his first cartoon to the *Daily Sketch* in the 1950s and later drew a series of long, thin cartoons for the paper, called "Tall Story", which were printed vertically along the gutter. In 1963 he became city cartoonist on the *Sunday Telegraph*, producing a series of pocket cartoons titled "Nine to Five". In 1966 he began the "Day by Day" series in the *Daily Telegraph* and also provided cartoons for the paper's Peterborough column, working alongside Basil Hone. Each cartoonist submitted three roughs, one of which would be selected for the next day's paper. He finally retired from the *Sunday Telegraph* in 1996.

Holte (Trevor Holder) b. 1941 British artist whose work has appeared in *Punch*, *Men Only* and *Reader's Digest*. He has also illustrated greeting cards, books and calendars, the last-named including the Esso calendar. Born in Birmingham, he left school at 15 and worked as a technical illustrator and graphic designer before becoming a full-time cartoonist in 1981. He drew *Punch's* final cover in 1992 before its relaunch in 1996. He works in pen and ink, watercolour, gouache and oils.

Honeysett, Martin b. 1943 After leaving art college, Hereford-born Honeysett travelled to New Zealand and Canada, performing a variety of jobs. On his return to England in 1969 he began submitting cartoons to papers and magazines including *Punch*, *Private Eye*, the *Spectator* and *Radio Times*. He has gone on to win several awards at international cartoon festivals and has illustrated a number of books, among them *Bert Feggs Nasty Book* by Terry Jones and Michael Palin and *The Queen and I* by Sue Townsend. Honeysett's distinctive sagging characters have been described as being in an advanced stage of elephantiasis, with clothing bought off the peg at rent-a-tent.

Husband, Tony b. 1950 A full-time cartoonist since 1984, he has a host of awards to his name. He specializes in sports cartoons – for *The Times* and the *Sunday Express* – and has twice been named Sports Cartoonist of the Year. He also created the ITV children's puppet and animation show *Round the Bend* and his books have been translated into German, Russian and Chinese.

Jolley, Richard b. 1967 Oxford-educated Jolley sold his first cartoon to Private Eye in 1990 and has since appeared in the likes of *Reader's Digest, New Statesman, The Oldie, Evening Standard*, and the *Spectator*. He has had an exhibition – "Eye Times" – at the National Portrait Gallery and has illustrated various books, including *Private Eye* annuals, *Spectator* cartoon books and *Great Sporting Failures*.

Khan, Ham b. 1957 He started his professional cartoon career in 1986 in Rio Cuarto, Argentina, and whilst he still lives in that country, his work has sold to the UK, Japan, South Africa, Norway and the US. A regular contributor to the *Observer*, he has also worked as a writer, designer and animator for Spitting Image Productions.

King, Jerry An army medic for three years before studying English at Ohio State University, King is one of America's foremost cartoonists, his fans including Bill Clinton. He has written and illustrated seven cartoon books, and has illustrated ten children's books and over 2,000 greeting cards. One of his cartoon characters has even been turned into a stuffed animal!

BIOGRAPHIES

Kirby, Vernon Cartoonist who contributed to *Punch* from 1963 to 1974.

Knife (Duncan McCoshan) b. 1961 Born in Scotland, McCoshan left school at 16 to work in a London bookshop and ended up staying there for 14 years. His cartoons have appeared in *Punch*, the *Spectator* and the *Guardian* and he has illustrated "The Naked Truth" series of children's books. His area of expertise is strip cartoons and since 1999 he and Jem Packer have drawn the popular "It's Grim Up North" strip in *Private Eye*.

Langdon, David b. 1914 After working as an architect, Londoner Langdon sold his first cartoon – a joke about Mussolini – to *Time and Tide* in 1936. The following year he was invited to contribute to *Punch* and during the war he produced a famous series of advertisements for London Transport entitled "Billy Brown of London Town." In 1948 he began a long association with the *Sunday Pictorial* (later renamed the *Sunday Mirror*) that only ended in 1990. Famed for his prolific output and wry slant on current affairs, he claims to have introduced the "open mouth" into humorous art, to indicate who is speaking.

Larry (Terry Parkes) 1927–2003 The son of a factory worker, Parkes acquired the nickname "Larry" while teaching at a school in Peterborough after the boys had seen Larry Parks in *The Al Jolson Story*. As a freelance cartoonist – notably for *Punch* – he became acknowledged as the master of the small domestic incident, frequently involving a big-nosed, middle-aged husband struggling to cope with household chores. He also became a regular illustrator of the *Private Eye* column "Colemanballs" and because most of his cartoons did not need captions, they appealed to readers throughout the world.

BIOGRAPHIES

Lowry, Ray b. 1944 As well as appearing in traditional cartoon outlets such as *Punch* and *Private Eye*, Lowry has enjoyed a long association with various strands of the British music press, particularly *Melody Maker* and *NME*, for whom, as an occasional writer, he conducted the first British interview with Cyndi Lauper. Has also worked for the *Guardian* and the *Observer*, specializing in cartoons on drink, drugs and rock 'n' roll.

McLachlan, Ed b. 1940 After attending Leicester College of Art, McLachlan sent a scrapbook of cartoons to *Punch* in 1961 and they bought one for seven guineas. Three weeks later, when they took seven of his cartoons, he decided that was the life for him. The move paid off. He became political cartoonist for the *Sunday Mirror* and has illustrated over 200 children's books. He also wrote and designed the ITV series *Simon and the Land of Chalk Drawings* and designed *Bangers and Mash* for the same company. Famed for his captionless cartoons, he likes to draw with ink and wash on board.

McMurtry, Stan (Mac) b. 1936 Edinburgh-born McMurtry worked as a film animator before becoming a freelance cartoonist in 1965. Three years later he was offered the job of topical cartoonist for the *Daily Sketch* and began signing his daily drawings "Mac". When the Sketch was absorbed by the *Daily Mail* in 1971, Mac began his association with that paper, seeing himself as a gently mocking cartoonist whose job "is to make the dreary news copy of the daily paper brighter by putting in a laugh". Revered as one of Britain's foremost cartoonists, since 1980 he has often included a miniature portrait of his blonde second wife Janet somewhere in his *Mail* cartoon.

BIOGRAPHIES

Mahood, Kenneth b. 1930 Born in Belfast, he had his first cartoon accepted by *Punch* at 18 and in 1960 was appointed the magazine's assistant art editor under William Hewison. In 1966 Mahood became the first political cartoonist on *The Times* and later worked for the *Evening Standard, Financial Times* and the *Daily Mail* for whom he drew its "Compact Cartoon". He once said of his topical work: "The important thing is to be witty and to make a comment at the same time, if possible."

Martin, Henry b. 1925 A graduate of the American Academy of Art, Chicago in the early 1950s, he drew for a number of publications before landing steady work with the *New Yorker*. He is best known for his "Good News/Bad News" strand, distributed nationally for 15 years, which placed particular emphasis on poking fun at the business world via stodgy businessmen, faceless office workers and megalomaniacal CEOs. Martin says of his work: "Ideas are the most important thing. The drawing is always secondary; the idea is important because a bad drawing can be carried by a good idea but not vice versa."

Matt (Matthew Pritchett) b. 1964 The son of journalist Oliver Pritchett, he began drawing cartoons in his spare time while working as a waiter in a pizza restaurant. On the death of Mark Boxer in 1988, he was offered the job of pocket cartoonist on the *Daily Telegraph* and by 2001 had drawn an estimated 2,500 pocket cartoons for the paper. In addition to collecting numerous awards, he was made an MBE in 2002. He says: "People tell me that my cartoons occasionally make political statements but all I am going for is the cheap laugh."

Matteson, Rip b. 1920 It was while growing up in Oakland, California that Rip Matteson decided to become an artist. He studied art in California and Rome and taught the subject until his retirement in 1983. Refusing to rest on his laurels, he promptly revived his interest in cartooning and saw his work published in *Saturday Review, Punch* and *Playboy.*

Mirachi, Joseph 1919–91 A native of Manhattan, he attended Art Students League after serving in the Second World War. He began drawing for the *New Yorker* in 1954 and the magazine printed 574 of his cartoons, many of them featuring feuding husbands and wives or bar room confessions.

Mishon, Joel b. 1970 After gaining a degree in History at the University of Birmingham, he had his first cartoon published in the *Spectator* in 1992. His work has since appeared in *Punch, Private Eye, Reader's Digest, The Times* and many more. He specializes in single panel gags and is cartoon editor at CartoonStock.com.

Mosedale, Mike After training in graphic design, he set up a graphic studio in London but found that he was becoming increasingly in demand to supply humorous illustrations. By the 1990s this had evolved into a full-time occupation for such publications as *The Times, Sunday Times, Evening Standard* and assorted trade magazines. His work is usually apolitical but topical.

Myers, David b. 1925 While still a student at art school, Myers managed to land a job as holiday stand-in for the *Daily Express*'s celebrated cartoonist Osbert Lancaster. As well as cartoons, he has designed hundreds of greeting cards, written scripts for comedians Dave Allen and Tommy Cooper, and in 1987 devised and wrote a BBC children's television series *Sebastian the Incredible Drawing Dog*. He never works with pencil roughs, once explaining: "I start work straight away with a pen, and if it doesn't show signs of going well, I tear it all up and start again."

BIOGRAPHIES

Naf (Andy McKay) Named Young Cartoonist of the Year in 2002 by the British Cartoonists' Association, Scotland-based McKay turned professional in 1997. His work has featured in, among others, *Private Eye*, *New Statesman*, *Reader's Digest* and *Punch*.

Newman, Nick b. 1958 Born in Kuala Lumpur, Newman went to Ardingly College, a boarding school in Sussex, where he first met his future writing partner Ian Hislop. After collaborating on school revues and an Oxford magazine called *Passing Wind*, they teamed up again for the ITV satirical puppet series *Spitting Image*. More recently they wrote the BBC series *My Dad's the Prime Minister*. Newman had drawn cartoons at school and sold his first to *Yachting Monthly* in 1976, thereafter contributing regularly to *Private Eye*, the *Sunday Times* and the *Guardian*, for whom he drew the "Megalomedia" strip with Ben Woolley.

Nick (Nick Hobart) b. 1939 Born in London, he worked for the Halifax Building Society before emigrating to the United States with his family. A *Punch* regular from 1976, he has also contributed to *The Wall Street Journal* and the *Spectator*. Specializes in religious and medical cartoons. Lives in Florida.

Orford, Fran b. 1957 Educated at Queens College, Oxford, and Leeds Business School, he was first published in *Punch* in 1986. The Yorkshire-based artist has since featured heavily in national newspapers and magazines, notably in the areas of law, finance and health. He lists his hobbies as "talking at length about things he doesn't understand and being scared of his daughters".

Pak (Peter King) A native of Liverpool, his distinctive cartoons have appeared in such places as *Private Eye*, the *Spectator*, *Punch*, the *Liverpool Daily Post* and *Reader's Digest*.

BIOGRAPHIES

Petty, Bruce Leslie b. 1929 Australian writer and illustrator who was appointed resident cartoonist on the *Sydney Daily Mirror* in 1963 and the newly established national daily, *The Australian*, from 1964 to 1973. He soon made his name for his penetrating visual comments on the involvement of Australia and the USA in the Vietnam War.

Pont (Graham Laidler) 1908–40 Celebrated *Punch* cartoonist who gently satirized the British character. Born in Newcastle-upon-Tyne, he started as a caricaturist at school where an unflattering likeness of the headmaster fell into the wrong hands leaving young Laidler unable to sit down for a few days. He went on to study architecture but ill health prevented him pursuing that career path and he took up cartooning instead. He first appeared in *Punch* in 1932 and for six years drew a strip cartoon for *Woman's Pictorial* chronicling the adventures of the Twiff family. A book *The British Carry On* featured a selection of his wartime cartoons drawn shortly before his death.

Pugh, Jonathan b. 1962 Educated at Oxford and Bath, he taught art and games at a prep school before trying his hand at cartooning. In 1995 he began drawing *The Times'* diary cartoon and the following year he became the paper's front-page pocket cartoonist. In 1997 he also became *The Times'* business cartoonist. He feels comfortable with the small format of the pocket cartoon, admitting that "anything much bigger and I'm drowning at sea."

Pyne, Ken b. 1951 The son of a boot-repairer, London-born Pyne had the distinction of being the youngest artist to be published in *Punch* in the twentieth century. He was just 16 at the time and he duly became a full-time freelance cartoonist four years later. He has since worked for *Private Eye* (providing the "Corporation Street" strip), *The Times*, the

Independent, New Statesman and the *Guardian.* Voted Joke Cartoonist of the Year for 1981, he has also illustrated the Good Beer Guide.

Raymonde, Roy b. 1929 Born in Grantham, Lincolnshire, he worked in the "cold, hard world" of advertising for ten years before becoming a freelance cartoonist and illustrator. His work has appeared in most British national newspapers, including regular features in the *Sunday Telegraph.* He has lectured in Korea and Japan.

Reeve, Tony A freelance cartoonist whose work has appeared in *The Times, Independent, Private Eye* and *Punch.* He draws the "Off Your Trolley" strip for *Private Eye* with Steve Way and created *Punch's* "On the Record" strip. He has also written for TV, radio and the stage and has illustrated greeting cards, children's books and company brochures.

Ross, Martin His work first appeared in *Punch* in 1990 and his quirky cartoons soon became a favourite with readers. Has been staff cartoonist on the *Yorkshire Evening Post,* drawing the "Ross's View" series. He also produces cartoons under the pen name "Guerre".

Saxon, Charles, 1920–88 Born in Brooklyn, he graduated from Columbia University in 1940 before working as an editor at Dell Publishing and serving as a bomber pilot in the Army Air Corps during the Second World War. In 1956 he became a cartoonist for the *New Yorker* and in a distinguished career went on to win the National Cartoonist Society's Advertising Award for 1977, its Gag Cartoon Award for 1980, 1986 and 1987, and the coveted Reuben Award for 1980.

Schwadron, Harley b. 1942 A philosophy graduate with an MA in journalism, New Yorker Schwadron worked as a newspaper reporter in Connecticut before becoming a full-time cartoonist. His cartoons have appeared in such diverse publications as the *Wall Street Journal* and *Playboy* and he has also illustrated more than 20 books.

Scully, William 1917–2002 Born in Ilkeston, Derbyshire, Scully worked as a pipe-tester in an ironworks and in an artificial silk factory before having his first cartoons accepted by the *Bystander*. During the Second World War he became art editor of an army magazine. He has done covers for *Punch* and contributed to *The New Yorker*. Fellow cartoonist Bill Hewison described Scully's work as "marvellously free and autographic but with a tight control over the use of tone. You are always aware of space in a Scully drawing."

Sewell (Patricia Carter) Her illustrations have appeared in the USA, Japan and the United Kingdom where her clients include *Punch*, *The Oldie* and Macmillan Publishing. Lives in Ipswich, Suffolk.

Siggs, Lawrie 1900–72 Buckinghamshire-born Siggs was training to be a wireless operator when he was struck down by appendicitis. While convalescing he met illustrator Albert Morrow who was in the same ward with a broken jaw. Although Siggs duly became a wireless operator with Marconi, Morrow's influence encouraged him to embark on a second career as a freelance commercial artist and cartoonist. He contributed to *Punch* for 35 years, his trademark being gentle cartoons featuring children and animals.

Sizemore, Jim b. 1937 He learned his trade at the Maryland, Institute of Art in the 1960s but did not become a professional cartoonist until 1981 when he sold his first work to TV Guide. His cartoons have since appeared everywhere from the *National Enquirer* to the *Wall Street Journal*. He has taught at universities and art museums as well as staging cartoon workshops for children in libraries and schools.

BIOGRAPHIES

Sprod, George 1919–2003 Adelaide-born Sprod volunteered for the Australian Army in the Second World War and spent three and a half years in a prisoner-of-war camp following the fall of Singapore. It was while being held captive that he began cartooning seriously. After the war he came to seek his fortune in London, *Punch* bought the first five drawings he showed them on the spot.

Starke, Leslie 1905–74. Began cartooning at the age of 36 although he had supplied caricatures to his local paper, the *Fife Herald*, as a youth. His drawing career took off during the Second World War thanks to several Ministry of Food commissions, including one – thought to be the world's largest – that was erected across London's County Hall.

Stott, Bill b. 1944 Born in Preston, Lancashire, he was a teacher for 30 years before taking up cartooning. He first appeared in *Punch* in 1978 and has also contributed to the *Daily Express, Amateur Photographer*, and *Yachting World*. He is also much in demand as an after-dinner speaker.

Taylor, J.W. 1908–85 John Whitfield Taylor contributed cartoons to *Punch* for nearly 50 years, mostly while serving as a school headmaster. Born in Stoke-on-Trent, Staffordshire, he has been hailed as one of the finest cartoonists of the twentieth century and a number of his cartoons are held in British Museum collections. His son, David Taylor, was editor of *Punch* 1986–89.

Thelwell, Norman 1923–2004 Thelwell sold his first drawings – of chickens – at the age of 15 and left school a year later to work as a junior clerk in a Liverpool office. After dabbling in cartooning during the war, he became a *Punch* regular from 1952 to 1977, contributing over 1,600 cartoons to the magazine, including 60 covers. He also worked for the *News Chronicle*, *Sunday Express* and *Tatler*. An accomplished draughtsman, Thelwell paid great attention to detail in his drawings and was particularly well known for his cartoons on English country life. "I'm more interested in the social than the political side of life," he revealed in 1965. "I have no axes to grind and no torches to bear. I just hope that my drawings provide reasonably pleasant entertainment."

Thomas Bros. Brothers Bill and Bob Thomas were born in Erie, Pennsylvania, where they made an early impression as artists by using a ladder to draw in crayon on their parents' living-room ceiling! Now based in Los Angeles, they have contributed to *Reader's Digest*, *National Enquirer*, *Women's World*, and specialist publications such as *Cat Fancy* and *Aquarium Fish Magazine*.

Thompson, Robert b. 1960 After gaining a degree in illustration at Leeds Polytechnic, Thompson became art editor of Camden Graphics, producing greeting cards. At the same time he freelanced as a cartoonist, selling his work to *Private Eye* and the *Spectator*, until in 1994 he went full-time as a freelance. His cartoons have since appeared in countless magazines and newspapers and he has also contributed ideas for ITV's animation series *2DTV*.

Tidy, Bill b. 1933 Tidy worked in a Liverpool shipping office and drew advertisements for *Radio Times* before becoming a professional cartoonist in 1957. Although he had no formal training, his output was prolific and he could turn out as many as 15 finished cartoons in a day. He became particularly well known for his strip cartoons "The Cloggies", which ran in *Private Eye* from 1967 to 1981, and "The Fosdyke Saga", which began in the *Daily Mirror* in 1971. He called the Fosdykes "my great standby, the rock on which my church is built" but when Robert Maxwell bought the *Mirror* in 1984, the popular strip was axed. Tidy refused to complete the final episode. Tidy's style has been influenced by the early work of Ronald Searle and like Jak, he draws hands in the Disney style – with only three fingers and a thumb.

Tombs, M.F. Tombs was a frequent contributor to *Punch* between 1960 and 1977.

Toos, Andrew b. 1958 A veteran American cartoonist, he was first published in the *Washington Post* in 1984 and his work has appeared in panel and strip form in hundreds of US newspapers such as the *Saturday Evening Post* and the *New Yorker* as well as in many of the leading consumer and technical magazines. He has also illustrated a number of books, including such diverse publications as *Conversation Strategies: Pair and Group Activities for Developing Communicative Competence.*

Twohy, Mike Raised in San Francisco, Twohy drew high-school sports cartoons for his local paper. After studying fine art at the University of California, he went freelance as a cartoonist, soon attracting the attention of *Saturday Review, TV Guide, Esquire* and, in 1980, the *New Yorker.* Recently his panel "That's Life" has been syndicated in the US. He gets most of his ideas in coffee shops and often works with a pet cockatiel on his shoulder. He does his work by hand, using pen tip in ink, and he colours his strips by hand with colour pens and watercolours – the old-fashioned way, he says, "like an eleventh century monk."

Way, Steve b. 1959 Born in Plymouth, Devon, his first published cartoon appeared in *National Student* in 1980. In 1989 he became cartoon editor of *Punch* and when the magazine closed, he co-founded the ill-fated venture *The Cartoonist* before becoming cartoon editor of *Maxim* in 1995. Two years later he returned to *Punch* in the magazine's

BIOGRAPHIES

reincarnation. His drawings have also appeared in *Private Eye*, the *Spectator*, the *Listener* and the *Observer*.

Whittock, Colin b. 1940 Editorial cartoonist on the *Birmingham Evening Mail* since 1969, he is also sports cartoonist for the *Sunday Mercury*. He provides the colour strip "Kev", which is signed "Andy", as it was originally a project for his son. Whittock has also contributed to *Punch*, *Daily Mirror*, *Tit-Bits* and various comics. He cites his influences as Leo Baxendale, Larry, Bill Tidy and Giles.

Wiles, A.F. b. 1926 Southampton-born Arnold Frederick Wiles worked in an aircraft factory during the Second World War and sold his first cartoon to *Punch* in 1943. He specialized in angling cartoons (having sold over 1,000 drawings on the subject) and has also designed humorous greeting cards for Royle, Raphael Tuck and Classic.

Williams, Mike b. 1940 Went to school in Liverpool with John Lennon and although he had no formal art training, he went on to work in a number of commercial illustration studios before becoming a freelance cartoonist and illustrator. His work has featured in many advertising campaigns, notably for BMW and Guinness. He was cartoon editor of *Punch* in 1997.

CREDITS

CARTOONSTOCK: Myke Ashley-Cooper 486; Bruce Baillie 394; Mike Baldwin 37, 129, 136, 142, 144, 155, 289; Neil Bennett 398; Philip Berkin 488; Chris Bray-Cotton 483; David Brown 149; Adey Bryant 337; Deacon 339; Stan Eales 39; Gilligan 133; Clive Goddard 283, 292, 334, 336, 338, 340, 342, 391, 396, 480; Grizelda 153; Ralph Hagen 132; Richard Jolley 489; Ham Khan 485; Jerry King 123, 124, 128; Knife 151; Ed McLachlan 140, 341; Joel Mishon 36, 285; Mike Mosedale 487; Naf 121, 335, 388; Fran Orford 138, 343; Pak 154; Jim Sizemore 287; Thomas Bros. 120; Andrew Toos 482, 484.

PUNCH: Ajay 206; Albert 72, 187, 231, 347, 430, 455; Anton 25, 96, 198, 241, 244, 270, 279, 286, 348; Sally Artz 42, 92; Nick Baker 44, 242, 293; Banx 29, 228, 230, 261, 318, 380, 384, 403, 410, 461, 463; Charles Barsotti 50, 191; Les Barton 12, 288; Neil Bennett 172, 262, 330; Bestie 464; Peter Birkett 213, 299, 306, 383, 429; Simon Bond 196; Hector Breeze 45, 48, 163, 390; Eric Burgin 189, 304; Tom Cheney 28; Chic 181; Clive Collins 98, 229, 278; Bernard Cookson 432, 465; Frank Cotham 30, 43, 46, 69, 71, 74, 81, 87, 164, 351; Roy Davis 109; Alan de la Nougerede 4, 134, 467; Geoffrey Dickinson 203; John Donegan 2, 13, 24, 49, 67, 68, 332, 366; Pete Dredge 99, 457; Riana Duncan 47, 52, 55, 73, 202, 260, 352, 364, 373, 382; Stan Eales 51, 236, 462; Eli 405, 418, 440; Michael ffolkes 6, 10, 34, 165, 168, 204, 227, 277, 350, 353, 355, 368, 378, 392, 436; Ed Fisher 53, 59, 226, 365, 417, 423, 481; Noel Ford 167, 190, 205, 209, 267, 356, 402, 407, 408, 441; André François 243; D.L. Ghilchik 271; Bud Grace 33, 188, 192, 245, 354, 399, 439, 468; Alex Graham 359; William Haefeli 173, 235, 310, 357, 360, 363, 369; David Haldane 7, 83, 161, 223, 250, 265, 361, 453, 469; Bud Handelsman 19, 54, 56, 219, 249, 269, 272, 282, 291, 322, 331, 358, 442; Merrily Harpur 89, 94, 97, 174, 178, 370, 416; Sidney Harris 63; David Hawker 471; Michael Heath 5, 57, 107, 111, 197, 200, 266, 305, 307, 309, 311, 381, 414, 435, 448; William Hewison 8; Gerard Hoffnung 160, 166;

CREDITS

Tony Holland 108; Holte 9, 23, 58, 116, 152, 156, 169, 184, 193, 208, 251, 255, 404, 425, 470; Martin Honeysett 11, 26, 76, 100, 145, 248, 268, 273, 395, 434; Tony Husband 17, 22, 77, 95, 101, 252, 274, 308, 329, 362, 466, 475; Vernon Kirby 32, 102; David Langdon 454; Larry 35, 38; Ray Lowry 78, 224, 263, 290, 296, 298, 300, 303, 313, 315; Ed McLachlan 14, 20, 64, 140, 158, 162, 194, 247, 264, 276, 341, 371, 393, 397; Stan McMurtry 106, 110, 112, 117, 143, 207, 216, 254; Kenneth Mahood 302, 321; Henry Martin 21, 65, 66, 70, 79, 246, 446; Matt 323, 459; Rip Matteson 80; Joseph Mirachi 150; David Myers 15, 62, 82, 141, 210, 376, 450, 473; Nick 122, 126, 170, 424, 472, 474, 476; Nick Newman 137, 379, 438; Bruce Leslie Petty 443; Pont 458, 460; Jonathan Pugh 239; Ken Pyne 75, 90, 139, 175, 201, 211, 253, 328, 377, 428, 477; Roy Raymonde 199; Tony Reeve 171, 176; Martin Ross 148, 180, 327, 415; Charles Saxon 346; Harley Schwadron 16, 86, 88, 113, 125, 127, 130, 179, 314, 326, 367, 372, 385, 437; William Scully 61, 85, 256, 325, 456; Sewell 320; Lawrie Siggs 185; Sam Smith 84; George Sprod 93, 177, 409; Leslie Starke 422, 449; Bill Stott 212; J.W. Taylor 103, 131, 312, 349, 389, 444; Norman Thelwell 3, 159, 237, 275; Robert Thompson 114, 234, 238, 240, 324; Bill Tidy 218, 220, 301; Tombs 433; Mike Twohy 319; Unknown 431; Steve Way 60, 104, 297, 419, 451; Colin Whittock 115; A.F. Wiles 186; Mike Williams 18, 27, 217, 221, 222, 225, 257, 284, 406, 411, 447, 452.

Front cover main image: © Terence Parkes, a.k.a Larry; www.larry.co.uk

Back cover image © Punch Ltd., www.punch.co.uk/Nick Hobart